William Bolcom

Borborygm

for Organ

ISBN 0-634-09680-X

EDWARD B.
MARKS MUSIC
COMPANY / EXCLUSIVELY DISTRIBUTED BY
HAL•LEONARD®
CORPORATION
7777 W. BLUEMOUND RD. P.O. BOX 13819 MILWAUKEE, WI 53213

borborygm: from Latin *borborygmus* (ultimately from Greek βορβοριγμός, or a rumbling of the bowels). (From the OED)

When William Albright died in 1998, his papers, musical and otherwise, were left in extreme disarray. I asked our assistant Carol Wargelin, herself a capable musician, to organize Albright's musical papers for the University of Michigan's Bentley Historical Library, and to save whatever sketches she could find for my use, as I intended to construct a memorial for Bill from them.

This is what I have done in fact; the opening and short connective parts are of my composition, which I have made to seem as integrated with the Albright material as possible. Since the sketches I used often trail off into nothing, I assume them to be unfinished pieces. Whenever I recognized a piece I knew in the sketches I did not use it, but this does not preclude the possibility that some musical material might also be found in a finished Albright work.

At times I used the Albright original verbatim—as it appeared in the sketch— but often I would take a small passage and develop or modify it to help construct a whole. Passages that were intended for organ often have registrations, mostly pedal indications, and the like (even in sketch form), and I have used them mostly as he left them. I have asked Marilyn Mason to help me make sense of it all, including my own impressionistically described registration desires.

—William Bolcom
July 7, 2001
Ann Arbor, Michigan

Commissioned by the American Guild of Organists
for the Biennial National Convention
Philadelphia, Pennsylvania, July 2002

PERFORMANCE NOTES

Accidentals obtain throughout a beamed group.   Unbeamed repeated notes continue the same accidental until interrupted by another note or rest.

The following symbols are used:

$\hat{?}$,   ,   Commas signify pauses, here shown in order of greatest to shortest duration.

ϕ Indicates free meter, measures contain an indeterminite number of beats. Events occur in time based on horizontal placement in a measure.

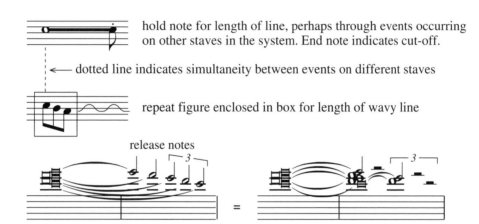

hold note for length of line, perhaps through events occurring on other staves in the system. End note indicates cut-off.

— dotted line indicates simultaneity between events on different staves

repeat figure enclosed in box for length of wavy line

release notes

REGISTRATION

Prepare: Great: Principal 8', Octave 4', 2', Mixtures, Ch./Gt.
Swell: Bourdon 16', Flutes 8'
Choir: Foundation 8', 4' with Reed 8'("nasty" stops)
Pedal: Bourdon 16', Flutes 8'

in memoriam William Albright

Borborygm

Edited by MARILYN MASON

WILLIAM BOLCOM (2001)
incorporating sketches of
WILLIAM ALBRIGHT

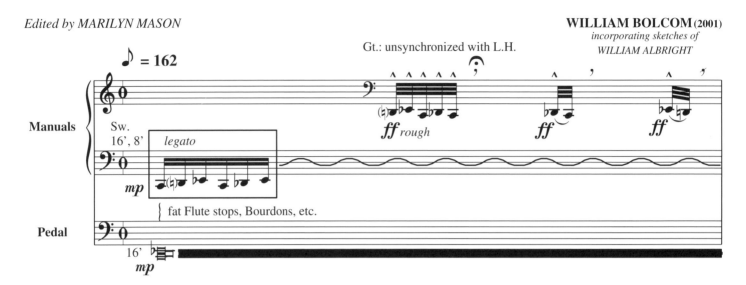

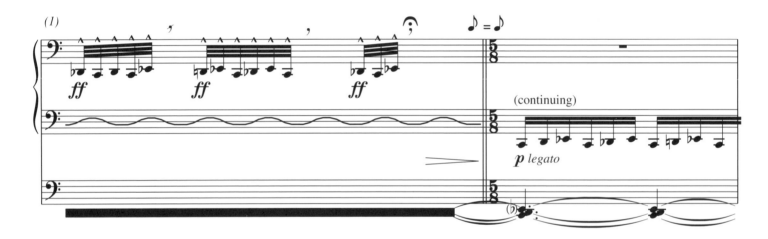

6

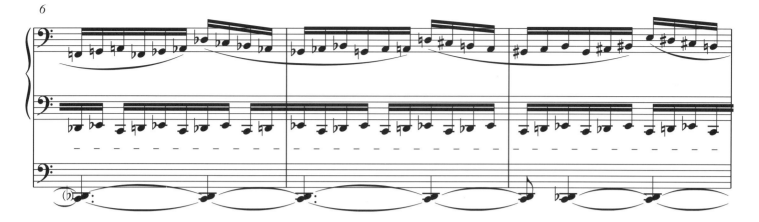

9

add stops, both manuals, as you can

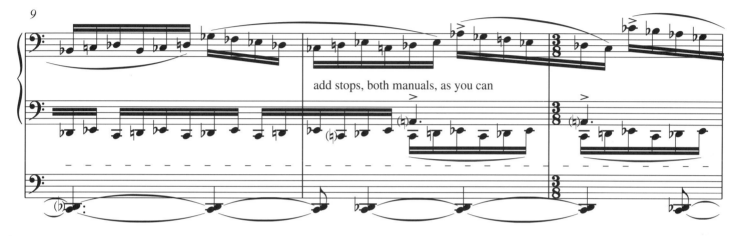

12

più cresc.

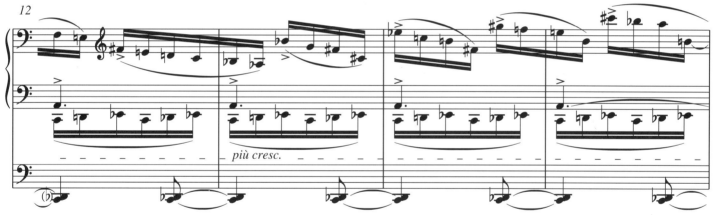

16

♩ = 44

Ped.: Fl. 16', 8', 4'

Ped.: reduce to open 16' Flute

dim. molto

BORBORYGM

with awesome stillness, floating in an uncertain light (W.A.)

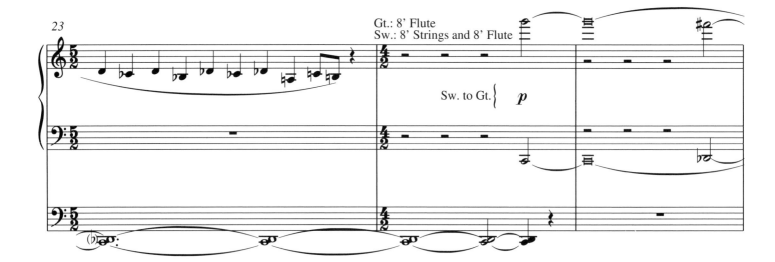

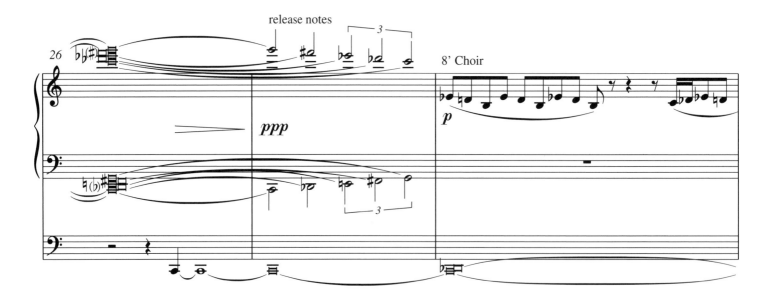

BORBORYGM

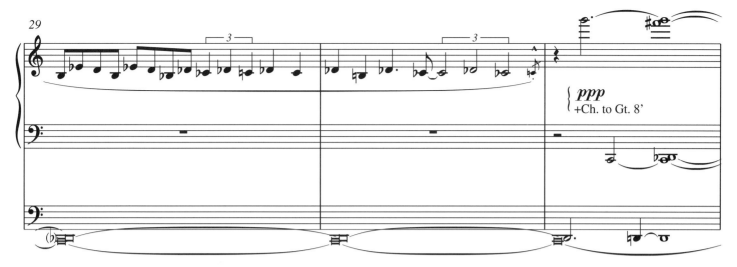

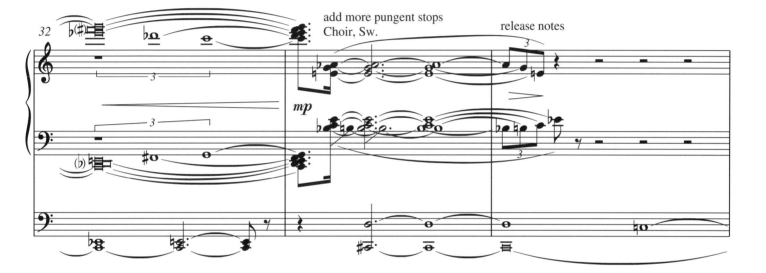

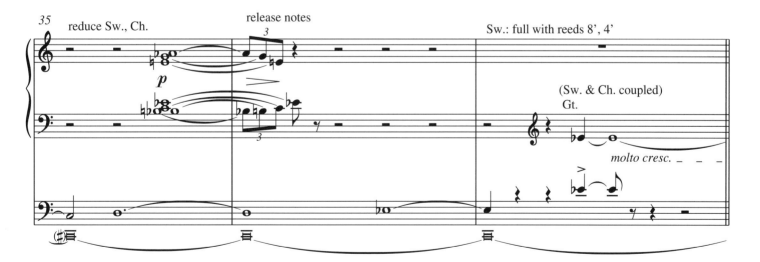

Faster ♩ = 96
Full Organ

BORBORYGM

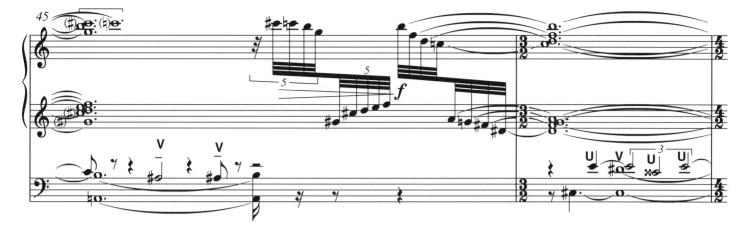

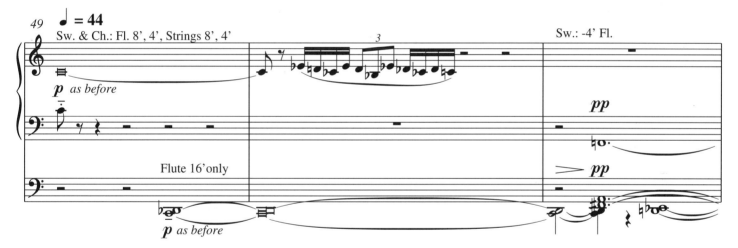

BORBORYGM

Choir: Fl. and Strings, 8' only
Sw.: Fls. 8', 2'; Gt. Fls. 8', 2'

BORBORYGM

explosive

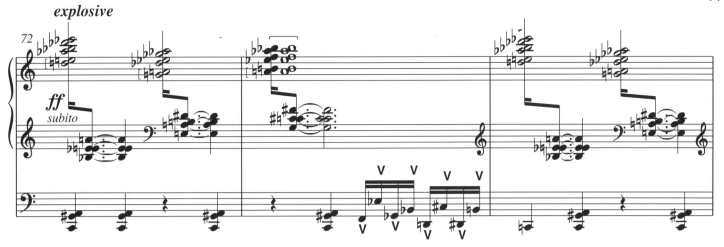

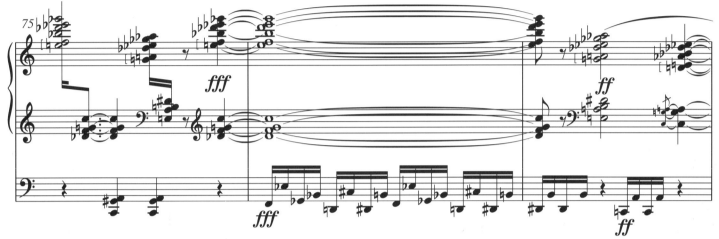

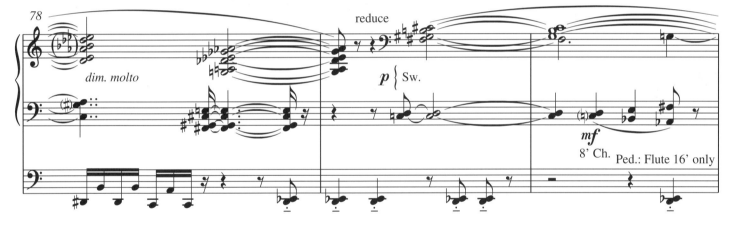

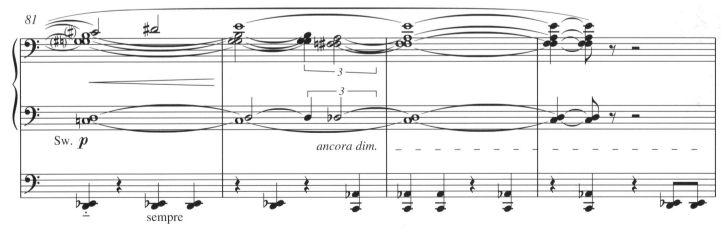

BORBORYGM

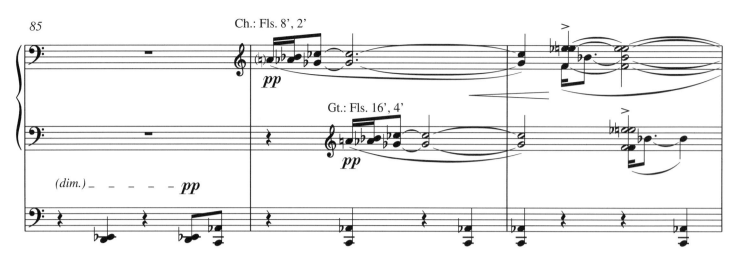

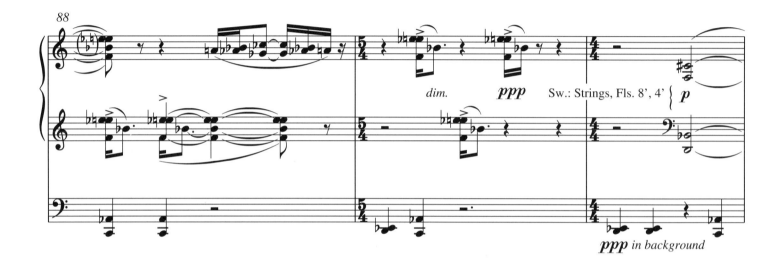

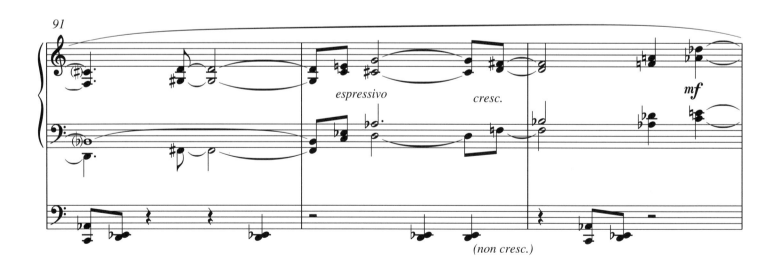

BORBORYGM

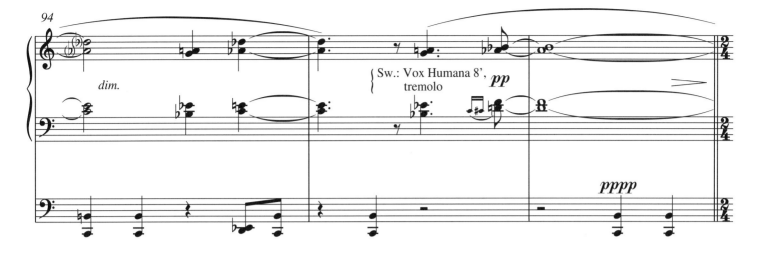

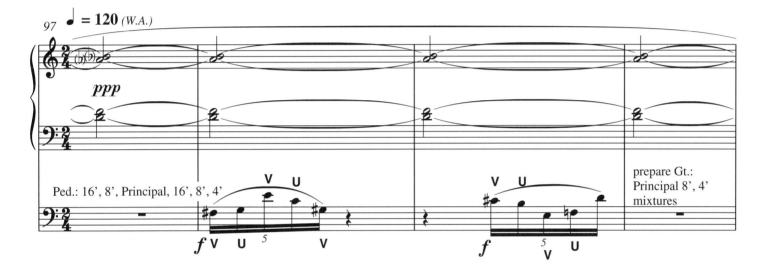

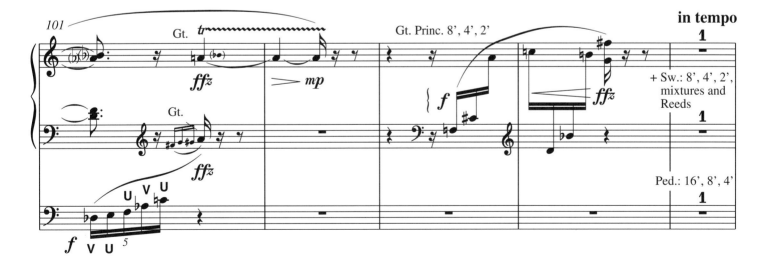

BORBORYGM

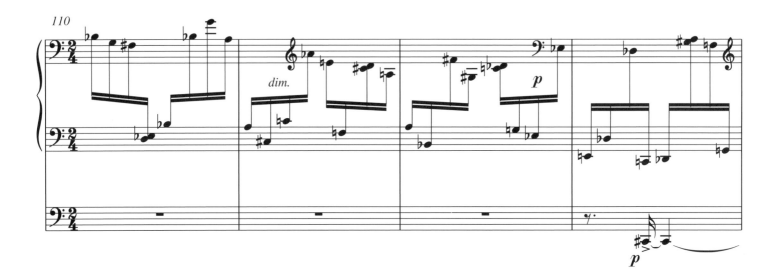

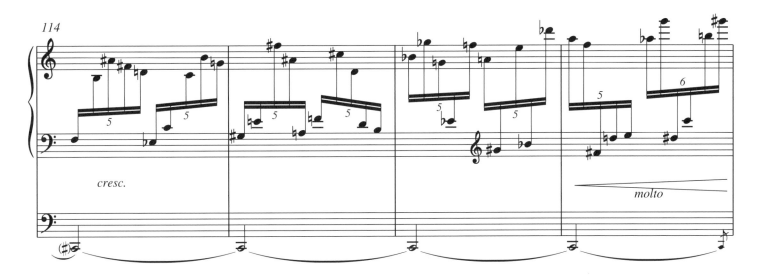

BORBORYGM

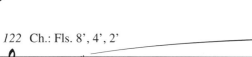

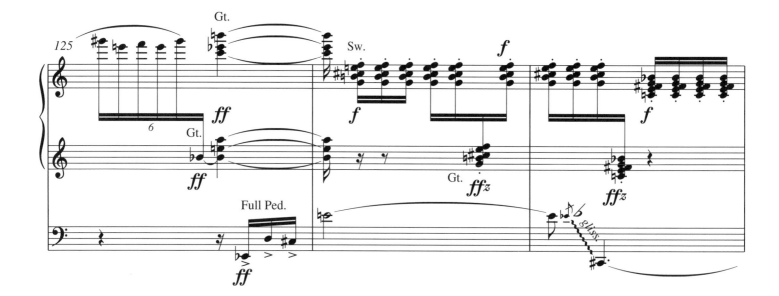

BORBORYGM

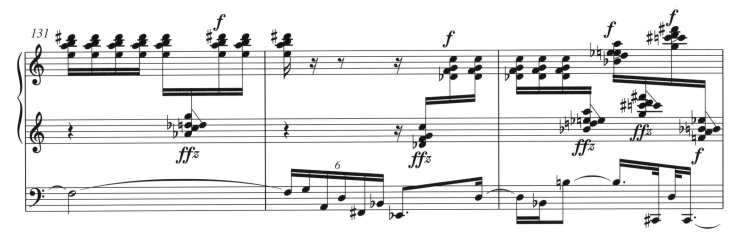

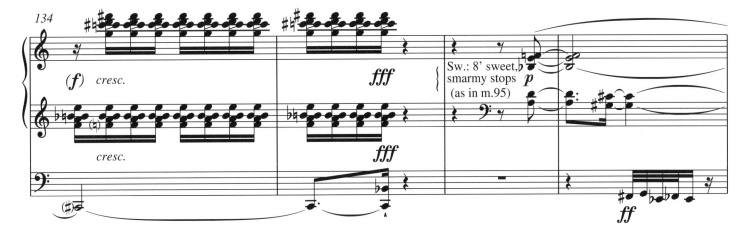

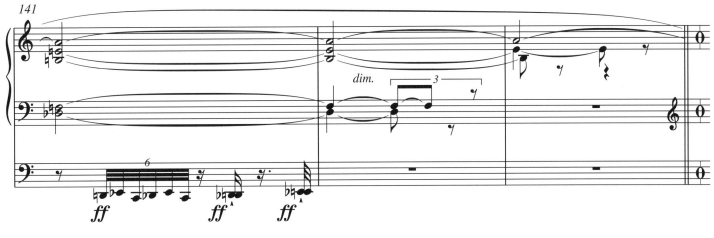

BORBORYGM

Slow

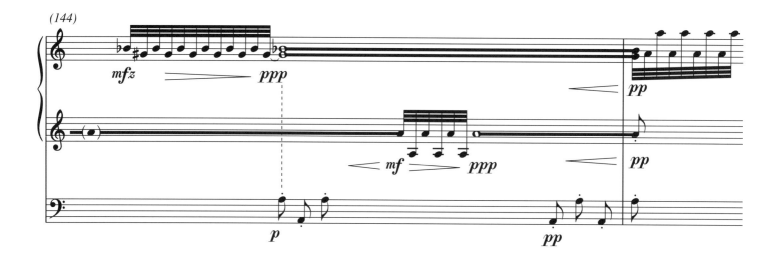

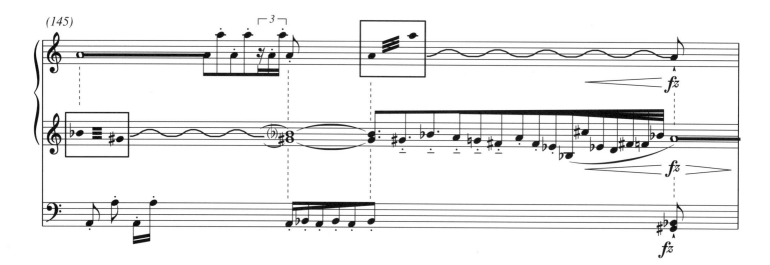

BORBORYGM

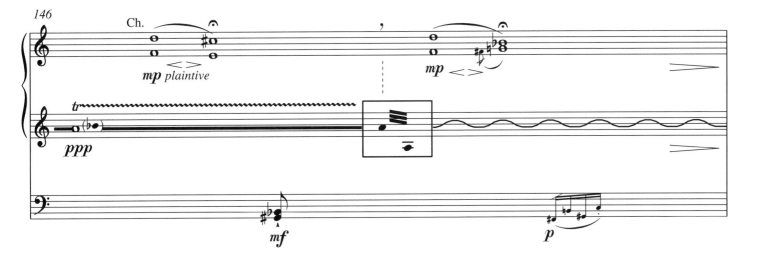

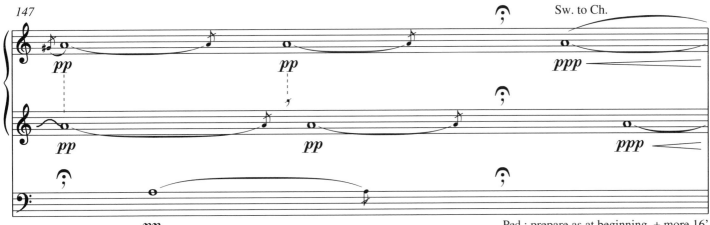

Ped.: prepare as at beginning, + more 16'

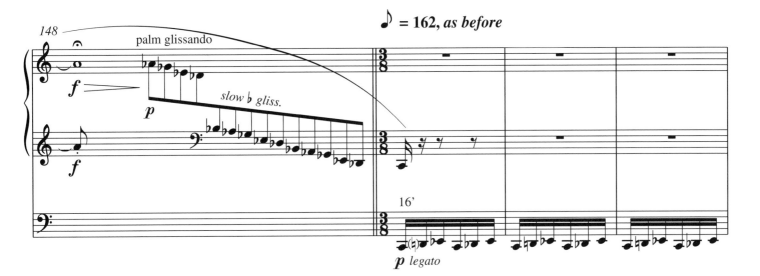

BORBORYGM

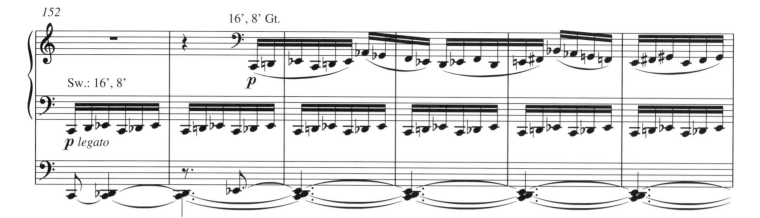

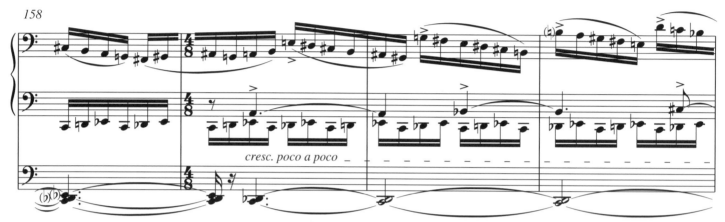

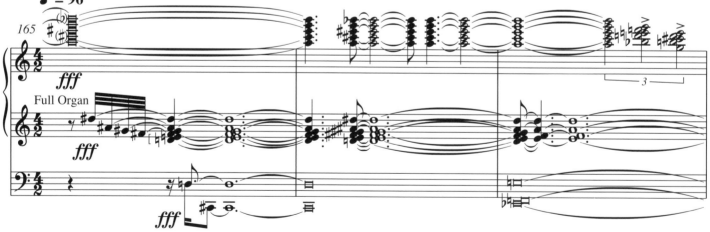

BORBORYGM

BORBORYGM

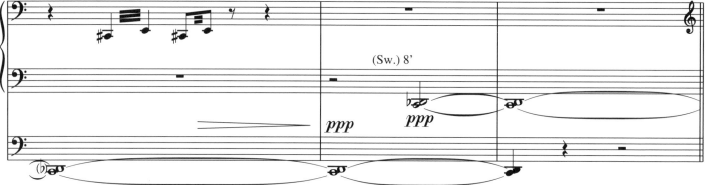

Envoi: Lamentoso ♩ = 52

Ch.: Reed 8', Fl. 8', Str. 8'

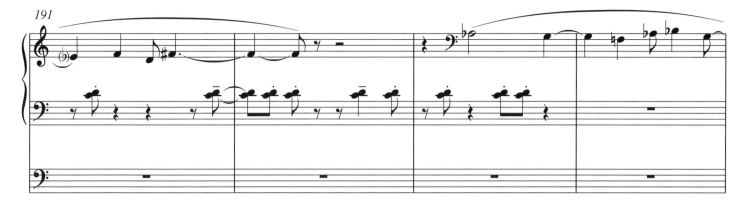

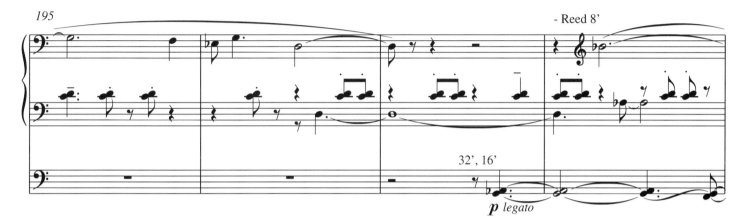

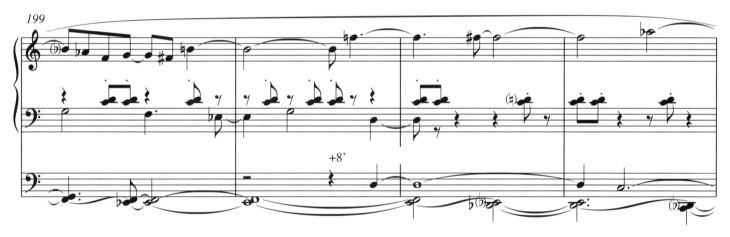

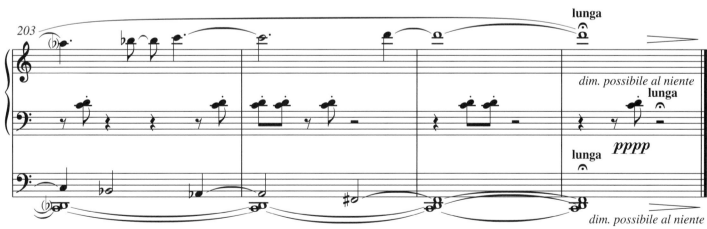

BORBORYGM

EDITOR'S NOTE

William Albright was an unusually talented student of mine at the University of Michigan; as my student he earned two degrees: B. Mus. (1966), and M.Mus. (1967), and later the DMA. (1970) in composition. I commissioned four works by him, studied them under his direction and premiered them in his presence. The red coffee pot he kept in his studio was given to me after his death September 17, 1998. It is a daily reminder of his presence, a souvenir of his labors as a composer, and our association as student, colleague, and friend.

Borborygm challenges the performer. It is unusual; perhaps it is unique. I know of no other such composition in our repertory: one composer's sketches developed and enhanced by another composer—a colleague—into something extraordinary. Bolcom's insight and imagination have produced an important work. Albright's originality, as suggested by his notes, tentative themes and musical ideas, here emerges into a coherent and impressive composition.

Albright's color and mood suggestions are in italics. My registration suggestions remain in normal type. Registrations of color and pitch are guidelines, but not obligatory.

A three-manual organ of 30–40 registers is probably needed to do justice to the work. An experienced organist may condense to two manuals. Organists who have instruments with a solo division will want to vary the individual sounds (those suggested on the choir, for example) with solo colors. The resources of the pipe–organ, the skill of the player, and the acoustics of the room all contribute to the successful creation and performance of this work.

—Marilyn Mason
August 29, 2001
Ann Arbor, Michigan